FüR IHN: A LOVER'S ODE

FROM FIRST GLANCE TO LAST GOODBYE

SWETHA SUNDAR

To him, who did show me the true meaning of love.
For six years of dreams, solitude, and all the things in between.
This book contains the echoes of us, every tear, every smile, and every memory captured in verse, even though we are no longer together.
You will always be a part of my heart's journey.

Contents

Foreword

Love is a beautiful and strange thing. Before we know it, it permeates every part of who we are. It often arrives subtly and when we least expect it. I knew for six years that love is real, imperfect, and not always simple. Even though our story comes to an end, its memory will live on in the hollows of my heart.

Für Ihn: A Lover's Ode is my attempt to preserve the quiet moments in between as well as the beauty, happiness, and heartache. These poems are fragments of a love that molded, transformed, and, in many ways, restored me to selfhood. They are pieces of my soul.

This is a celebration, a tribute to a time when everything seemed better, when love was a common language, and when each memory was a treasure rather than a burden. It is not a book about regret.

It is for him, the person who showed me what love is all about, and for everyone who has experienced the heartbreaking pain of a love that won't last but will always be significant.

To him: You will always have a place in my heart, even though we are no longer together. These poems are my way of honoring you for our love together.

Preface

Although love is not always permanent, its effects can be. Für Ihn: A Lover's Ode is the book that is the result of a six-year love that changed my life. It is a tribute to beginnings, to shared moments, and to the beauty of what was rather than a compilation of endings.

Memories such as simple pleasures, silent vows, unsaid griefs, and the silent power of a bond that seemed limitless at one juncture are woven throughout these poems. Composing this was a journey and a release, an effort to hold onto something valuable while also learning to let it go.

This isn't a book of regret. It honors love in all of its pure beauty, flaws, and rawness. It's for everyone who has ever clung to someone too carefully or let them go too quickly; it's for people who understand that love leaves an impression even when it can't last.

This book is written for him; you are the inspiration behind each line and the echo in each verse. I want to use these words to express my gratitude for everything—the lessons, the love.

And to the reader: I hope that this book touches your heart in the same way that these memories still touch mine.

Acknowledgements

To Sr.: For being the reason behind this journey, for the love that inspired these words, and for the memories that will forever hold a special place in my heart.

To Sudhar: Thank you for being my unwavering support, my confidant, and my constant source of encouragement through it all.

To Navee, Jeni, and Niya: You stood by me every step of the way, through the laughter and the tears. Your friendship has been a pillar of strength.

To Suvi and Deepthi: Thank you for believing in my voice and for pushing me to pen down my emotions. Your faith in me made this book possible.

To Swarnaa: For simply being there. Your presence has been a gift that words cannot fully capture.

To Mom: For existing, for your unconditional love, and for being my safe haven through everything.

To Lord Muruga: For the divine guidance and blessings that have lit my path, even in the darkest moments.

To all the readers: Thank you for believing in me and choosing to bring this book into your lives. Your support means the world, and I hope these poems speak to your hearts as deeply as they come from mine.

Finally, to the person I became through it all: this book is as much for you as it is for him. Thank you for finding the courage to embrace love, to endure its loss, and to transform it into something beautiful.

Prologue

Every relationship has a beginning, middle, and end. However, there are no precise definitions or boundaries elements that make up can be used to distinguish between the a relationship. They infuse together, intertwined in memories, fleeting encounters, and both spoken and unsaid words.

This book tells the tale of one of those loves—a love that was both painful and beautiful, short-lived and eternal. I traveled with him for six years, a journey that molded, educated, and ultimately aided in my individual growth. The love we once shared is still engraved in my soul in these verses, which are as much a part of me as the air I breathe, even though we are no longer on the same path.

Für Ihn: A Lover's Ode is more than just a book of verses. It is a letter to the past, a commemoration of the past, and a reminder that love endures even when the person we once loved is no longer with us. It discusses the bittersweet beauty of moving on without ever really letting go, the anguish of loss, and the delight of discovery.

Even though it can no longer be held, the pieces of a love that are preserved in these pages will never be forgotten. It is my present to him, to the person I once loved, and to everyone who has ever felt the profound, enduring effects of a love that was never intended to last.

1. The Moment I met You

It was 2018,
a momentary pass through the department door
your steps carried something unsaid,
your eyes, way to truths I couldn't look away from.
The way you talked,
like every word held its own space,
gentle, deliberate, but infinite in reach.
Every strand hair fell as if crafted by the wind itself,
an invitation to desire.
In that moment, I fell,
not into a moment,
but into you.

2. The Universe hidden in your Smile.

You were my senior,
and I was drawn to your orbit with every step I took.
Perfect attendance—not out of commitment,
but because it would allow me to see you and
catch a glimpse of the universe hidden in your smile.
You were a star of grace
The brilliance that I had never seen before;
I followed every word you spoke.
As though you were the sole truth
in a world that had just started to glow,
I watched in awe.

3. Love in Bloom

It was 25.11.2018, 11:59 PM,
when curiosity moved into courage.
I proposed, not knowing what would happen next,
but only sensing the spark of something new.
Months passed, and your yes came subtly,
not just in words, but through your actions,
the eye contacts, a quiet smile,
the ease of watching you from a distance.
In your company, the world faded,
leaving only us,
growing like wildflowers,
in the corridors of our classrooms,
rooted in joy.

4. Our Silent Language

We spoke in a tongue no one else knows,
a silent rhythm of eyes and smiles.
Even our eyes had their own dialect,
decoding truths only we could understand.
It was distinct, it was ours
a language painted with vibrant hues,
illuminating our world with endless love.
Being his junior meant everything,
to a universe made for us.
In that quiet, beautiful realm,
we needed no words - just ourselves.

5. Unspoken Storms

With unsaid words,

weighing down the clouds,

the sky between us grew darker.

A subdued tension developed,

with every pause

resonating like a thunder inside my heart.

Your eyes,

which had once been a place of refuge,

became unreadable mirrors.

The paths we created together,

blocking out by misunderstandings -

that piled up like debris.

Through the mist,

I reached for you,

but the storm held firm,

its winds bearing shards of uncertainty.

I could still feel

our anchor beneath the chaos,

steady as we waited for the skies to clear.

6. Falling Leaves

Our texts grew fewer,
and the calls were spaced out over the quiet.
Once unthinkable,
the distance between us -
now an unavoidable shadow.
Little things became sharp,
fights began to sprout from nothing.
Your voice changed,
from being melodic to being colder and stranger.
The vine of possessiveness,
strangled around my neck.
The ease we used to have —
hidden beneath uncertainties.
In the fall,
we were like trees,
with our love losing its leaves,
until only the bare branches were left.

7. Distance between Us

One and a half years of silent struggle,
with a never-ending pain deep inside.
Despite our best efforts,
the distance between us only widened.
The agony became a recurring theme in my life,
and I was unable to break free from its rhythm.
With the world inverted,
its shades faded to subdued shades of loss.
We walked through separation in search of hope,
a wound we couldn't accept.
Just the heavy silence of absence,
without any calls or words.
Time seemed to drag on exhaustingly,
as though the cosmos itself had stopped
and was waiting for us to return.

8. A Love That Could Not Be

For five years,
we experienced both calm and stormy times,
but even the most powerful tides eventually pass.
Slowly, we discovered that
not all stories are meant to be told.
This seems the last chapter -
the epic we wrote, line by line.
Reality persists - uncompromising,
whispering truths that we attempted to ignore.
Like the last notes of a song,
your voice and the echoes of "goodbye" linger.
Even though the pain is intense,
we let it go because,
we know that love, too, can also end.

9. Our Final Sunset

We reminisced about everything in the car,
including the beginning,
my first "I love you" whisper,
your smile, and my first gift.
All I saw was the past,
the location where we first revealed our truth,
even though the road extended ahead of us.
Tears fell silently,
as nostalgia clung to the air
like the aroma of a vanishing memory.
As the sunset painted the sky with farewells,
I held the poem I wrote for you,
a final letter to the love we once shared.

10. Echoes of Him

I recall your laughter,
as if the entire world had stopped for me.
Your generosity,
subtle yet profound,
and the way you seized a room.
In your eyes -
I saw the promise of tomorrow
a future we were never able to experience together.
The comfort of your voice,
the warmth of your touch,
lingers around my heart.
Even now,
your voice can still be heard,
whispering in the darkest corners of my heart.
I cherish everything about you,
including your love and beauty.

11. Pieces of Me

I'm grateful for the strength,
you left behind -
for making me into a resilient person.
You gave me the courage,
to remain upright even as the ground shook.
Thanks to him -
I found independence,
a voice I never knew was mine.
You taught me to have confidence,
to trust in myself,
to make decisions boldly.
I will always be thankful -
I am now a woman who recognizes her value.
Even if we are no longer together,
the parts of me that you shaped remain,
as evidence of our dynamic love.

12. Goodbye, My Love

Goodbye, my dear, as the stars take their place,
I send a wish to the universe for you.
May success find you in every aspect,
and your dreams bloom in a garden.
Take care of your dear mother,
the one who raised you.
May her days be brightened by your love,
her heart warmed by your care.
Be the wonderful person I always saw,
a garden of kindness where flowers grow freely.
May happiness follow you like sunlight,
and peace be the tune of your days.
You will forever be my 11:11 wish,
a secret prayer uttered to the stars.
I'm thankful for every moment we shared,
for the way your impact upon my life.
Though this is goodbye,
you'll always live in the quiet corners of my heart,
a memory painted in hues of gratitude and love.
Goodbye, my love—shine brightly, always.

Thank You

I would like to thank everyone who has read these words and joining me on this journey. I hope these pages help you piece together your own story and remind you that love, no matter how it unfolds or ends, is never really lost. It waited patiently to be remembered in the silent depths of our hearts.

www.ingramcontent.com/pod-product-compliance
Lightning Source LLC
Chambersburg PA
CBHW030511170726
47990CB00008BA/3151